Faith's Little Instruction Book For Mom

Harrison House
Tulsa, Oklahoma

Faith's Little Instruction Book For Mom
ISBN 0-89274-979-2
Copyright © 1996 by Harrison House, Inc.
P. O. Box 35035
Tulsa, Oklahoma 74153

This
Faith's Little Instruction Book For Mom

Presented to

_____

By

_____

Date

_____

Introduction

Faith's Little Instruction Book For Mom is a powerful collection of quotations by dynamic Spirit-filled women of our day. This book provides insights of wisdom for training children in areas such as building relationships, faith, learning responsibility, intercession and following the leading of the Holy Spirit.

Faith's Little Instruction Book For Mom is a treasury of truth and applicable knowledge that will renew your mind with the light of God's Word.

God has given parents tremendous responsibilities. Along with these responsibilities, however, God has given tremendous power to carry out what He requires. The power that God gives to parents is in His Word.

MARILYN HICKEY

Now unto him that is able to do exceeding abundantly above all that we ask or think, according to the power that worketh in us.

Ephesians 3:20

Our children and grandchildren are covered in our covenant with God. Everything God gives to me, He'll give to them. All protection that I have, He passes on to my family.

GLORIA COPELAND

Know therefore that the Lord thy God, he is God, the faithful God, which keepeth covenant and mercy with them that love him and keep his commandments to a thousand generations.

Deuteronomy 7:9

God commands us to be overcomers. The first place we must overcome (the Devil) is in our domains. We don't have authority over our neighbors. But we have authority at home.

BILLYE BRIM

Behold, I give unto you power to tread on serpents and scorpions, and over all the power of the enemy: and nothing shall by any means hurt you.

Luke 10:19

*T*each (your children) **properly in the Word and live the Word before them. They will be a pleasure to you.**

PAT HARRISON

*P*rovoke not your children to wrath: but bring them up in the nurture and admonition of the Lord.

Ephesians 6:4

God is concerned about the peace of your children. He wants to bless you and your family, but you must choose the blessing. You must choose life for yourself and for your children. And life comes through God's Word.

MARILYN HICKEY

And all thy children shall be taught of the Lord; and great shall be the peace of thy children.

Isaiah 54:13

It's amazing to see the results of applying the Word of God to the lives of our children. He will perform His Word over our children, but we must first take the time to sow it into them.

LYNN BRACO

The sower soweth the word. And these are they which are sown on good ground; such as hear the word, and receive it, and bring forth fruit, some thirtyfold, some sixty, and some an hundred.

Mark 4:14,20

When we teach our children properly
in the Word and live the Word before them,
we are fulfilled with beautiful children.

PAT HARRISON

As arrows are in the hand of a mighty man; so are
children of the youth. Happy is the man that hath
his quiver full of them: they shall not be ashamed,
but they shall speak with the enemies in the gate.

Psalm 127:4,5

Regardless of the age of your children or how far they have drifted, you can still maintain your position as guard and release God's power in their lives.

MARY JEAN PIGEON

... *The effectual fervent prayer of a righteous man availeth much.*

James 5:16

Children don't understand the unseen
forces that are coming against them.
So it's your responsibility to stand against
those forces on their behalf.

GLORIA COPELAND

Wherefore take unto you the whole armour
of God, that ye may be able to withstand in the
evil day, and having done all, to stand.

Ephesians 6:13

When you rule God's way, your children
will not only respect and obey, but
they will desire to please you.

SHARON DAUGHERTY

*For whom the Lord loveth he correcteth;
even as a father the son in whom he delighteth.*

Proverbs 3:12

It **is important for parents to live the Christian life before their children.**

ORETHA HAGIN

Do all things without murmurings and disputings:
That ye may be blameless and harmless,
the sons of God, without rebuke, in the midst
of a crooked and perverse nation, among
whom ye shine as lights in the world.

Philippians 2:14, 15

Once you get things straight between you and your husband, you'll have a lot more power where your children are concerned.

GLORIA COPELAND

Likewise, ye husbands, dwell with them according to knowledge, giving honour unto the wife, as unto the weaker vessel, and as being heirs together of the grace of life; that your prayers be not hindered.

1 Peter 3:7

*P*arents should not only teach their children, but they should set a godly example in the home.

ORETHA HAGIN

Be ye followers of me, even as I also am of Christ.

I Corinthians 11:1

No matter what you say to your children,
they are going to follow your example —
whether good or bad.

PAT HARRISON

So speak ye, and so do, as they that shall
be judged by the law of liberty.

James 2:12

Children are like wet cement; early impressions made on them are long lasting.

BEVERLY LaHAYE

And these words, which I command thee this day, shall be in thine heart: And thou shalt teach them diligently unto thy children, and shalt talk of them when thou sittest in thine house, and when thou walkest by the way, and when thou liest down, and when thou risest up.

Deuteronomy 6:6,7

Children will do what you say when they're young, but they'll do what you do when they're grown!

ROXANNE SWANN

Train a child in the way he should go, and when he is old he will not turn from it.

Proverbs 22:6 NIV

While your children are growing up, they might forget some of the sermons you've preached, or act like they're not interested in the things of God. However, they will never forget your example.

GLORIA COPELAND

Train up a child in the way he should go: and when he is old, he will not depart from it.

Proverbs 22:6

Children will usually become what their parents are.

ORETHA HAGIN

Therefore be imitators of God, as beloved children.

Ephesians 5:1 RSV

*O*ur attitudes toward the children and the constancy of living a godly life day by day are what will stay in their minds and hearts.

NANCY COLE

*F*or bodily exercise profiteth little: but godliness is profitable unto all things, having promise of the life that now is, and of that which is to come.

1 Timothy 4:8

Your example will go a lot further than your words.

GLORIA COPELAND

Those things, which ye have both learned, and received, and heard, and seen in me, do: and the God of peace shall be with you.

Philippians 4:9

*If a husband and wife are loving
and kind toward each other, their children
will grow up to be loving and kind too.*

ORETHA HAGIN

*And this is his commandment, That we should
believe on the name of his Son Jesus Christ, and
love one another, as he gave us commandment.*

1 John 3:23

As we impart into our children by the Spirit of God, they will comprehend great spiritual truths at an early age. We do not impart what we know, we impart who we are.

CHERYL SALEM

Which things also we speak, not in the words which man's wisdom teacheth, but which the Holy Ghost teacheth; comparing spiritual things with spiritual.

1 Corinthians 2:13

From the time you hold your child in your arms, you begin to whisper in its ear, "God is your Creator and your Father. Jesus is the Lord of our home." That child's spirit is alive unto God from the time he is born into this earth.

PAT HARRISON

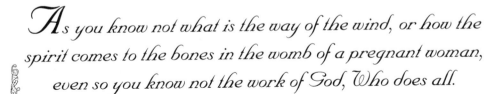

As you know not what is the way of the wind, or how the spirit comes to the bones in the womb of a pregnant woman, even so you know not the work of God, Who does all.

Ecclesiastes 11:5 AMP

If you begin to confess what God's Word says about your home life and your family members, you will begin to see that nothing is impossible because you will come under the authority of the Word.

MARILYN HICKEY

But what saith it? The word is nigh thee, even in thy mouth, and in thy heart: that is, the word of faith, which we preach.

Romans 10:8

There is one important thing about applying the Word. You must look into it, see who it says you are and — despite all natural appearances to the contrary — you must believe it.

LYNNE HAMMOND

But the man who looks intently into the perfect law that gives freedom, and continues to do this, not forgetting what he has heard, but doing it — he will be blessed in what he does.

James 1:25 NIV

Our words and our mouths
create the atmosphere that we're
going to have in our homes.

BRENDA TIMBERLAKE

A man's belly shall be satisfied with the fruit of his mouth; and with the increase of his lips shall he be filled. Death and life are in the power of the tongue: and they that love it shall eat the fruit thereof.

Proverbs 18:20,21

The words we speak, the prayer we pray, and the songs we sing create the atmosphere of our home. Make your house a haven your family enjoys coming home to.

ROXANNE SWANN

Through wisdom is an house builded; and by understanding it is established: And by knowledge shall the chambers be filled with all precious and pleasant riches.

Proverbs 24:3,4

As a parent, continually share the Word with your children.

PAT HARRISON

And these words, which I command thee this day, shall be in thine heart: And thou shalt teach them diligently unto thy children, and shalt talk of them when thou sittest in thine house, and when thou walkest by the way, and when thou liest down, and when thou risest up.

Deuteronomy 6:6,7

If you are not giving the Word
to your children, you are not building
your house in wisdom and instruction.

MARILYN HICKEY

*Every wise woman buildeth her house: but
the foolish plucketh it down with her hands.*

Proverbs 14:1

If you train your children and put the Word into them when they are young, they may make some mistakes as they are growing up, but they won't be swept away by the world.

ORETHA HAGIN

That we henceforth be no more children, tossed to and fro, and carried about with every wind of doctrine, by the sleight of men, and cunning craftiness, whereby they lie in wait to deceive; But speaking the truth in love, may grow up into him in all things, which is the head, even Christ.

Ephesians 4:14, 15

The challenge we face as parents is to consistently put the Word of God into our hearts and confess it with our mouths.

CHERYL SALEM

We having the same spirit of faith, according as it is written, I believed, and therefore have I spoken; we also believe, and therefore speak.

2 Corinthians 4:13

*Pray God's Word over your husband,
over yourself, and over your children.*

SHARON DAUGHERTY

*And take the helmet of salvation, and the sword
of the Spirit, which is the word of God: Praying
always with all prayer and supplication in the Spirit,
and watching thereunto with all perseverance
and supplication for all saints.*

Ephesians 6:17,18

You can be instrumental in making
your husband and children successful,
productive, happy people!

BEA BASANSKY

*Her children arise up, and call her blessed; her
husband also, and he praiseth her. Many daughters
have done virtuously, but thou excellest them all.*

Proverbs 31:28, 29

Fill your house with the Word, and the house will fill up with riches and wealth.

MARILYN HICKEY

Through wisdom is an house builded;
and by understanding it is established:
And by knowledge shall the chambers be
filled with all precious and pleasant riches.

Proverbs 24:3,4

You must know it is God's will to heal you.
Until this fact is settled in your mind and spirit,
you cannot approach healing without being
double-minded and wavering.

GLORIA COPELAND

My son, attend to my words; incline thine ear unto my sayings. Let them not depart from thine eyes; keep them in the midst of thine heart. For they are life unto those that find them, and health to all their flesh.

Proverbs 4:20-22

Intercession for our husband and for our children for the needs in their lives is a God-given responsibility to a wife and mother.

BEA BASANSKY

Likewise the Spirit also helpeth our infirmities: for we know not what we should pray for as we ought: but the Spirit itself maketh intercession for us with groanings which cannot be uttered. And he that searcheth the hearts knoweth what is the mind of the Spirit, because he maketh intercession for the saints according to the will of God.

Romans 8:26,27

Not only can you and I speak the Word of God over our own lives, but we can be an effective intercessor by speaking and praying the Word of God over the lives of others.

JOYCE MEYER

And take the helmet of salvation, and the sword of the Spirit, which is the word of God: Praying always with all prayer and supplication in the Spirit, and watching thereunto with all perseverance and supplication for all saints.

Ephesians 6:17,18

Get the Word into your children when they are young.

MARILYN HICKEY

And that from a child thou hast known the holy scriptures, which are able to make thee wise unto salvation through faith which is in Christ Jesus.

2 Timothy 3:15

It is important that from the time you are aware of conception to speak the Word to your child.

PAT HARRISON

Death and life are in the power of the tongue: and they that love it shall eat the fruit thereof.

Proverbs 18:21

You can begin to make your faith effectual
for your household by saying what
God's Word says about them.

MARILYN HICKEY

That the communication of thy faith may
become effectual by the acknowledging of every
good thing which is in you in Christ Jesus.

Philemon 1:6

It is imperative that we say the same thing that God says about our children.

JERI WILLIAMS

Can two walk together, except they be agreed?

Amos 3:3

We have all heard our words come out of our children's mouths! Let it be the Word of God coming out of our mouths that they repeat.

CHERYL SALEM

For verily I say unto you, That whosoever shall say unto this mountain, Be thou removed, and be thou cast into the sea; and shall not doubt in his heart, but shall believe that those things which he saith shall come to pass; he shall have whatsoever he saith.

Mark 11:23

We must teach our children to reverence the presence of God.

JERI WILLIAMS

And when the Lord saw that he turned aside to see, God called unto him out of the midst of the bush, and said, Moses, Moses. And he said, Here am I. And he said, Draw not nigh hither: put off thy shoes from off thy feet, for the place whereon thou standest is holy ground.

Exodus 3:4,5

*A*s Christian parents, we must seek God daily for wisdom in every decision that surfaces as a result of simply being a parent!

MARGARET HICKS

The young lions do lack, and suffer hunger: but they that seek the Lord shall not want any good thing.

Psalm 34:10

Spend time daily with the Lord. Fellowship, ask, pray, seek and come out of that time with Him equipped for the job at hand.

JOYCE MEYER

One thing have I desired of the Lord,
that will I seek after; that I may dwell in the
house of the Lord all the days of my life, to behold
the beauty of the Lord, and to inquire in his temple.

Psalm 27:4

When you are honest with yourself
and God, He can create a fresh clean heart
and renew a steadfast spirit within you.

CATHY DUPLANTIS

*Create in me a pure heart, O God,
and renew a steadfast spirit within me.*

Psalm 51:10 NIV

If Jesus had to take time alone
with God, then we surely need to.

SHARON DAUGHERTY

And it came to pass in those days,
that he went out into a mountain to pray,
and continued all night in prayer to God.

Luke 6:12

If you are tender toward God,
you'll be tender toward people,
including your husband and children.

SHARON DAUGHERTY

*And herein do I exercise myself, to have always a
conscience void of offence toward God, and toward men.*

Acts 24:16

Set the right example and walk in love toward your spouse and your children.

ORETHA HAGIN

That they may teach the young women to be sober, to love their husbands, to love their children.

Titus 2:4

It is important to set priorities in your life.
Establish what things are of most importance,
then let everything else fall into its right place.

SHARON DAUGHERTY

Brethren, I count not myself to have apprehended:
but this one thing I do, forgetting those things which
are behind, and reaching forth unto those things which
are before, I press toward the mark for the prize of the
high calling of God in Christ Jesus.

Philippians 3:13, 14

God wants you to get with Him yourself on a daily basis. That's what will change you.

JOYCE MEYER

When thou saidst, Seek ye my face; my heart said unto thee, Thy face, Lord, will I seek.

Psalm 27:8

I have found that if you let Jesus guide your life, and you walk closely with Him, you will set the right example for your children, and things will go well for you and your children.

ORETHA HAGIN

Observe and hear all these words which I command thee, that it may go well with thee, and with thy children after thee for ever, when thou doest that which is good and right in the sight of the Lord thy God.

Deuteronomy 12:28

Your children need true love and understanding. The only way to give them that love and understanding is to give them God's Word.

PAT HARRISON

And we have known and believed the love that God hath to us. God is love; and he that dwelleth in love dwelleth in God, and God in him.

1 John 4:16

As we become parents, we begin to see a tiny glimpse of the true love the Father God has for us.

CHERYL SALEM

Behold, what manner of love the Father hath bestowed upon us, that we should be called the sons of God: therefore the world knoweth us not, because it knew him not.

1 John 3:1

The greatest thing that you can give your children is love, because love encompasses the whole spectrum of life.

ROXANNE SWANN

And now abideth faith, hope, charity, these three; but the greatest of these is charity.

1 Corinthians 13:13

Children who aren't shown any love
will grow up not knowing how to give
or receive love properly.

ORETHA HAGIN

*Love worketh no ill to his neighbour:
therefore love is the fulfilling of the law.*

Romans 13:10

God desires tender compassion to flow from a mother's great love for her family.

JERI WILLIAMS

And Jesus, when he came out, saw much people, and was moved with compassion toward them, because they were as sheep not having a shepherd: and he began to teach them many things.

Mark 6:34

*P*arents should show God's love to their
children, but they should show natural love,
too, because children need affection.

ORETHA HAGIN

*S*o, being thus tenderly and affectionately desirous
of you, we continued to share with you not only
God's good news (the Gospel) but also our own lives
as well, for you had become so very dear to us.

1 Thessalonians 2:8 AMP

The Spirit of God will draw your family through His love. But you can't love others if you don't let God love you first.

JOYCE MEYER

Beloved, if God so loved us, we ought also to love one another.

1 John 4:11

Our children need "quality" time where there is interaction between them and their parents.

SHARON DAUGHERTY

That our sons may be as plants grown up in their youth; that our daughters may be as corner stones, polished after the similitude of a palace.

Psalm 144:12

If your relationship with your children is good at home, then they will relate to others well, too.

SHARON DAUGHERTY

That they may teach the young women to be sober, to love their husbands, to love their children.

Titus 2:4

Nothing will contribute more to a child's well-being and adjustment than growing up in a home where love and appreciation between the parents are evident.

MARGARET HICKS

Nevertheless let every one of you in particular so love his wife even as himself; and the wife see that she reverence her husband.

Ephesians 5:33

A husband and wife who don't show love to each other are setting the wrong example for their children.

ORETHA HAGIN

And walk in love, as Christ also hath loved us, and hath given himself for us an offering and a sacrifice to God for a sweetsmelling savour.

Ephesians 5:2

One of the best things that parents can do for their children is to develop the right atmosphere in the home, or what I call, "warm the nest."

MARILYN HICKEY

Finally, brethren, whatsoever things are true, whatsoever things are honest, whatsoever things are just, whatsoever things are pure, whatsoever things are lovely, whatsoever things are of good report; if there be any virtue, and if there be any praise, think on these things. Those things, which ye have both learned, and received, and heard, and seen in me, do: and the God of peace shall be with you.

Philippians 4:8,9

There is nothing closer to our hearts than the desire to see children raised in an atmosphere of love, being taught about God and His love.

MARGARET HICKS

Provoke not your children to wrath: but bring them up in the nurture and admonition of the Lord.

Ephesians 6:4

The responsibility for how your child turns
out rests on your shoulders, parents.

PAT HARRISON

*Train up a child in the way he should go:
and when he is old, he will not depart from it.*

Proverbs 22:6

We are accountable to God for our children's total well-being and satisfaction.

JERI WILLIAMS

Obey them that have the rule over you, and submit yourselves: for they watch for your souls, as they that must give account, that they may do it with joy, and not with grief: for that is unprofitable for you.

Hebrews 13:17

As Christian parents, we have the ability and privilege to impart spiritual truths into our children's spirits.

CHERYL SALEM

Making request, if by any means now at length I might have a prosperous journey by the will of God to come unto you. For I long to see you, that I may impart unto you some spiritual gift, to the end ye may be established.

Romans 1:10, 11

It is of paramount importance as
mothers that we teach our children
the attributes of the Holy Spirit.

JERI WILLIAMS

*She opens her mouth in skillful and godly
Wisdom, and on her tongue is the law of kindness
[giving counsel and instruction].*

Proverbs 31:26 AMP

*What an awesome responsibility
we have in fashioning that which
God has placed in our hands.*

JERI WILLIAMS

*Hath not the potter power over the clay,
of the same lump to make one vessel unto honour,
and another unto dishonour?*

Romans 9:21

*C*hildren always make their needs
known, and an attentive heart on
our part will supply that need.

JERI WILLIAMS

*B*ut my God shall supply all your need according
to his riches in glory by Christ Jesus.

Philippians 4:19

God knows how to deliver your children.
Do your part and trust Him to do His.

GLORIA COPELAND

The Lord knoweth how to deliver the godly out of temptations, and to reserve the unjust unto the day of judgment to be punished.

2 Peter 2:9

As a mother, my job is to take care of the possible and trust God with the impossible.

RUTH BELL GRAHAM

And Jesus looking upon them saith, With men it is impossible, but not with God: for with God all things are possible.

Mark 10:27

*P*arenting is not something to be palmed off onto counselors, day-care workers, coaches or teachers. Children need parents first, then all other adults in their network of support.

MARY JEAN PIGEON

*S*he riseth also while it is yet night, and giveth meat to her household, and a portion to her maidens.

Proverbs 31:15

We must not become deafened to the "cries"
of our children because we are so caught
up in attending our own needs.

JERI WILLIAMS

*Hereby perceive we the love of God, because
he laid down his life for us: and we ought to
lay down our lives for the brethren.*

1 John 3:16

Raising children is a big responsibility, but with the Lord to help you, you can be successful.

ORETHA HAGIN

I can do all things through Christ which strengtheneth me.

Philippians 4:13

It is the private time you spend
with God, just loving Him and letting
Him love you, that's going to cause you to
grow up and be strong in your spirit man.

JOYCE MEYER

*Abide in me, and I in you. As the branch
cannot bear fruit of itself, except it abide in
the vine; no more can ye, except ye abide in me.*

John 15:4

Motherhood is a full-time job that never ends!

NANCY COLE

*Who can find a virtuous woman? for her price
is far above rubies. She riseth also while it is
yet night, and giveth meat to her household,
and a portion to her maidens.*

Proverbs 31:10, 15

God wants to help us in our God-given task of being a mother. He wants us to gird ourself with strength from Him, because that's the only way we can be that "virtuous mother."

ROXANNE SWANN

*She girdeth her loins with strength,
and strengtheneth her arms.*

Proverbs 31:17

God longs for us to know life, not mere
existence. He longs for us to know the
beauty of motherhood, not merely
the hard work and inevitable pain.

BEVERLY LaHAYE

*The thief cometh not, but for to steal, and to kill,
and to destroy: I am come that they might have life,
and that they might have it more abundantly.*

John 10:10

God created you to have children, so He has given you all the knowledge and ability you need.

PAT HARRISON

And God blessed them, and God said unto them, Be fruitful, and multiply, and replenish the earth, and subdue it: and have dominion over the fish of the sea, and over the fowl of the air, and over every living thing that moveth upon the earth.

Genesis 1:28

There is a rest available in our homes that is paramount to our survival as wives and mothers.

JERI WILLIAMS

Let us labour therefore to enter into that rest, lest any man fall after the same example of unbelief.

Hebrews 4:11

*O*ur families are in covenant relationship with God, and we overcome the Devil by the blood of the Lamb and by the word of our testimony.

MARILYN HICKEY

And they overcame him by the blood of the Lamb, and by the word of their testimony; and they loved not their lives unto the death.

Revelation 12:11

We parents need to pray a wall of protection around our children and grandchildren, commanding Satan to stay away from our children in Jesus' name.

EVELYN ROBERTS

And these signs shall follow them that believe; In my name shall they cast out devils; they shall speak with new tongues.

Mark 16:17

If you are a believer and you're willing to trust God for the deliverance and salvation of your children, you will not be disappointed.

GLORIA COPELAND

For the scripture saith, Whosoever believeth on him shall not be ashamed.

Romans 10:11

And when he had brought them into his house, he set meat before them, and rejoiced, believing in God with all his house.

Acts 16:34

Don't ever be satisfied until your children are Spirit filled.

MARILYN HICKEY

For the promise is unto you, and to your children, and to all that are afar off, even as many as the Lord our God shall call.

Acts 2:39

Any sacrifice you might make for your children is not too great a price to pay to be sure your children have the best life possible.

ORETHA HAGIN

For God so loved the world, that he gave his only begotten Son, that whosoever believeth in him should not perish, but have everlasting life.

John 3:16

The joys of motherhood far outweigh the burden of responsibility.

NANCY COLE

A woman when she is in travail hath sorrow, because her hour is come: but as soon as she is delivered of the child, she remembereth no more the anguish, for joy that a man is born into the world.

John 16:21

If you teach your children the
difference between right and wrong,
they will be able to make right decisions
when they are out on their own.

ORETHA HAGIN

*Train a child in the way he should go,
and when he is old he will not turn from it.*

Proverbs 22:6 NIV

If you do not discipline your children,
you do not love them.

PAT HARRISON

*He that spareth his rod hateth his son: but he
that loveth him chasteneth him betimes.*

Proverbs 13:24

Consistent godly discipline is not an option but a commandment.

JERI WILLIAMS

Chasten thy son while there is hope, and let not thy soul spare for his crying.

Proverbs 19:18

Discipline begins at home, not in the church or school.

ORETHA HAGIN

Correct thy son, and he shall give thee rest;
yea, he shall give delight unto thy soul.

Proverbs 29:17

Be careful to discipline in love and
with a gentle tongue.

PAT HARRISON

*A man's belly shall be satisfied with the
fruit of his mouth; and with the increase
of his lips shall he be filled.*

Proverbs 18:20

We must be consistent with our children in giving them equal amounts of love and discipline.

MARGARET HICKS

Chasten thy son while there is hope,
and let not thy soul spare for his crying.

Proverbs 19:18

There is a proper way to discipline —
not through anger, but through love.

PAT HARRISON

*Foolishness is bound in the heart of a child;
but the rod of correction shall drive it far from him.*

Proverbs 22:15

I believe it's better to teach children the difference between right and wrong than it is just to teach them a lot of do's and don'ts.

ORETHA HAGIN

Train up a child in the way he should go [and in keeping with his individual gift or bent], and when he is old he will not depart from it.

Proverbs 22:6 AMP

*P*art of your responsibility as a parent is to put up a shield of faith that will help protect your children from the influence of the Evil One.

GLORIA COPELAND

*A*bove all, taking the shield of faith, wherewith ye shall be able to quench all the fiery darts of the wicked.

Ephesians 6:16

Children left to themselves, without rules or regulations, become insecure.

MARY JEAN PIGEON

The rod and reproof give wisdom: but a child left to himself bringeth his mother to shame.

Proverbs 29:15

Children need and actually want some boundaries. This creates security in their lives.

SHARON DAUGHERTY

Correct thy son, and he shall give thee rest; yea, he shall give delight unto thy soul.

Proverbs 29:17

We must discipline children so that they can lead orderly fruitful lives where their spirit man rules and reigns.

JERI WILLIAMS

*Correct thy son, and he shall give thee rest;
yea, he shall give delight unto thy soul.*

Proverbs 29:17

*I*t's our responsibility to "provoke" our children to love. Stir up feelings inside of them to do good, to please you and to please Jesus.

ROXANNE SWANN

And let us consider one another to provoke unto love and to good works.

Hebrews 10:24

Check up on yourself to make sure
you are walking in love and disciplining
according to the Word.

PAT HARRISON

*And walk in love, as Christ also hath loved us,
and hath given himself for us an offering and a
sacrifice to God for a sweetsmelling savour.*

Ephesians 5:2

Give your children counsel and instruction
with words of kindness.

ROXANNE SWANN

*She openeth her mouth with wisdom;
and in her tongue is the law of kindness.*

Proverbs 31:26

God desires that you be gentle with
your children, not only in your mannerisms,
but with your tongue.

PAT HARRISON

*Pleasant words are as a honeycomb,
sweet to the mind and healing to the body.*

Proverbs 16:24 AMP

The highest reward we can give
our children is praise.

ROXANNE SWANN

*Pleasant words are as an honeycomb,
sweet to the soul, and health to the bones.*

Proverbs 16:24

By **disciplining our children correctly,
we not only develop a parent-child relationship,
but a friendship as well.**

PAT HARRISON

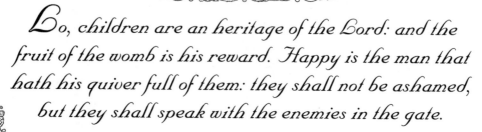

*Lo, children are an heritage of the Lord: and the
fruit of the womb is his reward. Happy is the man that
hath his quiver full of them: they shall not be ashamed,
but they shall speak with the enemies in the gate.*

Psalm 127:3,5

Our responsibilities for loving and giving ourselves to our children as a mother are great. Our actions may determine the degree our child learns to love and trust God!

ROXANNE SWANN

Yet you brought me out of the womb; you made me trust in you even at my mother's breast.

Psalm 22:9 NIV

Don't get too busy. If you don't have time to pray and spend time with God, then you are too busy.

JOYCE MEYER

As the hart panteth after the water brooks,
so panteth my soul after thee, O God.
My soul thirsteth for God, for the living God:
when shall I come and appear before God?

Psalm 42:1,2

God understands the life of a mother who is making the effort to seek Him. You can seek Him all through the day. He's listening.

SHARON DAUGHERTY

Hear, O Lord, when I cry with my voice: have mercy also upon me, and answer me. When thou saidst, Seek ye my face; my heart said unto thee, Thy face, Lord, will I seek.

Psalm 27:7,8

When children see that they are doing what the Word says, and that the Word works, they will have a desire to do those things.

PAT HARRISON

But be ye doers of the word, and not hearers only, deceiving your own selves.

James 1:22

Whether you believe it or not, your children will do what you do.

ORETHA HAGIN

Those things, which ye have both learned, and received, and heard, and seen in me, do: and the God of peace shall be with you.

Philippians 4:9

If you teach your children properly and show God's love to them when they're young, they won't ever stray very far from the Lord, even when they are older.

ORETHA HAGIN

Therefore shall ye lay up these my words in your heart and in your soul, and bind them for a sign upon your hand, that they may be as frontlets between your eyes. And ye shall teach them your children, speaking of them when thou sittest in thine house, and when thou walkest by the way, when thou liest down, and when thou risest up.

Deuteronomy 11:18,19

The way parents talk to their children is vital to their upbringing. Harsh words can eventually cause a child's will to be broken.

PAT HARRISON

There is that speaketh like the piercings of a sword: but the tongue of the wise is health.

Proverbs 12:18

Our **essential responsibility is to initiate a love for God's Word and impart wisdom in our children.**

JERI WILLIAMS

These commandments that I give you today are to be upon your hearts. Impress them on your children. Talk about them when you sit at home and when you walk along the road, when you lie down and when you get up.

Deuteronomy 6:6,7 NIV

We need to have the Word flowing throughout our homes.

PAT HARRISON

My son, attend to my words; consent and submit to my sayings. Let them not depart from your sight; keep them in the center of your heart. For they are life to those who find them, healing and health to all their flesh.

Proverbs 4:20-22 AMP

Every day you should speak the Word, pray the Word, love the Word and honor the Word. The Word of God is the two-edged sword that is your weapon of offense with which you are able to defend yourself.

JOYCE MEYER

For the word of God is quick, and powerful, and sharper than any twoedged sword, piercing even to the dividing asunder of soul and spirit, and of the joints and marrow, and is a discerner of the thoughts and intents of the heart.

Hebrews 4:12

Remember the Word works, and no matter how the circumstances may seem, your child will follow after what he has been taught.

PAT HARRISON

While we look not at the things which are seen, but at the things which are not seen: for the things which are seen are temporal; but the things which are not seen are eternal.

2 Corinthians 4:18

The Spirit of God is calling us to whet
our children's appetite for the things of God
and to urge on their mind by frequent
admonitions in the Scriptures.

JERI WILLIAMS

*And these words, which I command thee this day,
shall be in thine heart: And thou shalt teach them
diligently unto thy children, and shalt talk of them when thou
sittest in thine house, and when thou walkest by the way,
and when thou liest down, and when thou risest up.*

Deuteronomy 6:6,7

Your children will respect you and will learn positive habits and attitudes from you when your words and actions are a reflection of your love for God and His Word.

ORETHA HAGIN

Jesus said unto him, Thou shalt love the Lord thy God with all thy heart, and with all thy soul, and with all thy mind.

Matthew 22:37

Children will learn to forgive their parents and see the good in them when parents model and actively teach a positive attitude.

MARY JEAN PIGEON

And be ye kind one to another, tenderhearted, forgiving one another, even as God for Christ's sake hath forgiven you.

Ephesians 4:32

*B*e big enough to say to your child, "I'm sorry."

PAT HARRISON

*Submitting yourselves one to another
in the fear of God.*

Ephesians 5:21

You have to be big enough to let your kids know that you make mistakes too. Children have an easy time following our example when they see us repent for our mistakes.

ROXANNE SWANN

If we confess our sins, he is faithful and just to forgive us our sins, and to cleanse us from all unrighteousness.

1 John 1:9

Cultivating discipline in your child will cause him to understand authority and have respect for you, for himself and for the people and things around him.

PAT HARRISON

For whom the Lord loveth he chasteneth, and scourgeth every son whom he receiveth. If ye endure chastening, God dealeth with you as with sons; for what son is he whom the father chasteneth not?

Hebrews 12:6,7

It is so important to provide a happy home for your family. If your children grow up in a good home atmosphere, they will always have pleasant memories of home even as adults.

ORETHA HAGIN

She looketh well to the ways of her household, and eateth not the bread of idleness.

Proverbs 31:27

The manner in which we deal with situations at home will affect our children outside the home.

ROXANNE SWANN

He must manage his own family well and see that his children obey him with proper respect. (If anyone does not know how to manage his own family, how can he take care of God's church?)

1 Timothy 3:4,5 NIV

The parent trains through instruction and example.

SHARON DAUGHERTY

Do not irritate and provoke your children to anger [do not exasperate them to resentment], but rear them [tenderly] in the training and discipline and the counsel and admonition of the Lord.

Ephesians 6:4 AMP

Good teaching begins at home and reaches out into every area of our lives.

PAT HARRISON

Who can find a virtuous woman? for her price is far above rubies. She openeth her mouth with wisdom; and in her tongue is the law of kindness.

Proverbs 31:10,26

When your children come to you for answers, get your Bible and express the answer in the simplest way.

PAT HARRISON

Thy testimonies are wonderful: therefore doth my soul keep them. The entrance of thy words giveth light; it giveth understanding unto the simple.

Psalm 119:129,130

If the Word can hold the sun and moon in place, then I believe it can answer any need that you and I may have in our families.

MARILYN HICKEY

So shall my word be that goeth forth out of my mouth: it shall not return unto me void, but it shall accomplish that which I please, and it shall prosper in the thing whereto I sent it.

Isaiah 55:11

*I*n teaching a child how to believe, one of the most vital points is to teach them you never quit believing.

CHERYL SALEM

*L*et us hold fast the profession of our faith without wavering; for he is faithful that promised.

Hebrews 10:23

Your children learn more of your faith during the bad times than they do during the good times.

BEVERLY LaHAYE

That the trial of your faith, being much more precious than of gold that perisheth, though it be tried with fire, might be found unto praise and honour and glory at the appearing of Jesus Christ.

1 Peter 1:7

Three essential ingredients your child needs in order to be a success in life: encouragement, praise and affection.

ROXANNE SWANN

Pleasant words are as a honeycomb,
sweet to the mind and healing to the body.

Proverbs 16:24 AMP

*A*s a wife, mother and woman, you need
to plant seeds of love, praise, truth, confidence,
admiration and so forth in your home.

BEA BASANSKY

*Be not deceived; God is not mocked: for whatsoever
a man soweth, that shall he also reap.*

Galatians 6:7

Always assure your children when they are very young that they will amount to something.

ORETHA HAGIN

Truly I tell you, whoever says to this mountain, Be lifted up and thrown into the sea! and does not doubt at all in his heart but believes that what he says will take place, it will be done for him.

Mark 11:23 AMP

Our children are not failures! They just need parents who will love them enough to believe in them!

ROXANNE SWANN

Wherefore receive ye one another, as Christ also received us to the glory of God.

Romans 15:7

It **is our responsibility before God to create in our children a thirst and a desire to fulfill their individual gifts.**

JERI WILLIAMS

That our sons may be as plants grown up in their youth; that our daughters may be as corner stones, polished after the similitude of a palace.

Psalm 144:12

Each child has a gift within him that will cause him to excel in life. But that gift must be channeled by discipline, love, understanding and knowledge.

PAT HARRISON

Train up a child in the way he should go: and when he is old, he will not depart from it.

Proverbs 22:6

You cannot give your child too much encouragement and praise. Children thrive on the encouragement and praise you give them.

ROXANNE SWANN

A man shall be satisfied with good by the fruit of his mouth: and the recompence of a man's hands shall be rendered unto him.

Proverbs 12:14

Each child has their own way of doing things, their own personality, their own strengths, their own weaknesses. This diversity is what makes children fun, challenging, frustrating, and wonderful. God loves individuals, not clones.

CHERYL SALEM

I will praise thee; for I am fearfully and wonderfully made: marvellous are thy works; and that my soul knoweth right well.

Psalm 139:14

How beautiful it is to believe God —
take Him at His Word — say what He says —
and agree with Him that our children are an
inheritance from Him and His reward to us.

JERI WILLIAMS

*Behold, children are a heritage from the
Lord, the fruit of the womb a reward.*

Psalm 127:3 AMP

Children want to give of themselves to us just as we want to give of ourselves to them.

CHERYL SALEM

Lo, children are an heritage of the Lord: and the fruit of the womb is his reward.

Psalm 127:3

The Father God can pour His love
into our hearts through our children
and minister to us in great ways.

CHERYL SALEM

*And I have declared unto them thy name,
and will declare it: that the love wherewith thou
hast loved me may be in them, and I in them.*

John 17:26

Enjoy your children — God gave them to you to make you laugh!

JEANNE CALDWELL

Happy is the man that hath his quiver full of them: they shall not be ashamed, but they shall speak with the enemies in the gate.

Psalm 127:5

*Loving your children will enable
them to be lovers.*

ROXANNE SWANN

We love him, because he first loved us.

1 John 4:19

The love from our children is irreplaceable, yet the love of the Father God is greater still.

CHERYL SALEM

Behold, what manner of love the Father hath bestowed upon us, that we should be called the sons of God: therefore the world knoweth us not, because it knew him not.

1 John 3:1

God is so gracious to His children and is concerned about every area of our lives.

BETTY PRICE

He predestined us to be adopted as his sons through Jesus Christ, in accordance with His pleasure and will.

Ephesians 1:5 NIV

"In Christ," let us release that abundant life and usher our families into heavenly places.

JERI WILLIAMS

The thief cometh not, but for to steal, and to kill, and to destroy: I am come that they might have life, and that they might have it more abundantly.

John 10:10

We often fail to realize that redemption has power over the destruction the Devil tries to bring on our children's lives.

GLORIA COPELAND

Christ hath redeemed us from the curse of the law, being made a curse for us: for it is written, Cursed is every one that hangeth on a tree.

Galatians 3:13

The way a child turns out reflects on the parents.
So make sure that you are walking in love.

PAT HARRISON

*For all the law is fulfilled in one word, even in this;
Thou shalt love thy neighbour as thyself.*

Galatians 5:14

*I*n order to converse with God, we must learn to speak as God speaks, because we are told that if we ask anything according to His will He hears us.

GERMAINE COPELAND

And this is the confidence that we have in him, that, if we ask any thing according to his will, he heareth us.

1 John 5:14

*W*e will see victories in our family when we stay in the Word, study the Word and utilize the Word in prayer.

MARY JEAN PIGEON

My son, attend to my words; incline thine ear unto my sayings. Let them not depart from thine eyes; keep them in the midst of thine heart. For they are life unto those that find them, and health to all their flesh.

Proverbs 4:20-22

*S*top looking at your family from your own limited perspective and start seeing it as God sees it — as a powerhouse.

GLORIA COPELAND

*H*ow should one chase a thousand, and two put ten thousand to flight, except their Rock had sold them, and the Lord had shut them up?

Deuteronomy 32:30

References

The Harrison House Vision

Proclaiming the truth and the power
Of the Gospel of Jesus Christ
With excellence;

Challenging Christians to
Live victoriously,
Grow spiritually,
Know God intimately.